HEARING VOICES

Michael McIrvin

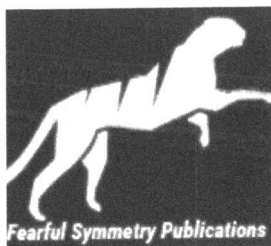

Fearful Symmetry Publications

ISBN: 978-1-7341970-0-6

First Edition
00 01 02 03   7   6   5   4   3   2   1

Acknowledgments

Versions of some of the poems in this collection were first published in the following: *Aesthetica, Ascent Aspirations, Calamity Jane, Caper Journal, Grasslimb, Misfit Magazine, Muse Apprenticeship Guild, Pedestal Magazine, Pemmican, Roux Magazine, Sulphur River Literary Review, Tamafyr Mountain Poetry, The Great American Poetry Show.*

"The Naming" first appeared in *Comparative Literature and Culture* (Special Edition: Representing Humanity in an Age of Terror) as part of an article titled "Poetry and the Aesthetic of Morality."

Other Books by Michael McIrvin

Optimism Blues: Poems Selected and New

The Book of Allegory

Dog

Lessons of Radical Finitude

Love and Myth

The Blue Man Dreams the End of Time (novel)

Déjà vu and the Phone Sex Queen (novel)

Whither American Poetry (essays)

...the voices of shadows reach for me
(from "A Religious Sadness")

I didn't want to listen but the wind, the sea,
howled the world's blood-stained torments.
(from "A Sacred Madness")

For Leonard Cirino (1943-2012)
poet, publisher, and friend

Contents

Hearing Voices

High Plains Book of the Dead

Noir Love Song

Lessons

Poet in (Perpetual) Wartime

Hearing Voices

Hearing Voices

...angels are voices beyond us
in us...
          Albert Goldbarth

...in Hölderlin's language,
the world's night is the holy night.
          Martin Heidegger

Voices reverberate in our blood like the big bang,
the vestigial hum of the desire for union.
The great *in-here* with the great *out-there*.
Equal vastnesses few have plumbed to the bottom
and survived to sing. So we attempt to tame
this urge by naming it. *Love,* we say. *God.*
The Heartstrings-of-Divine-Joy-Plucked.
Then we cower at thought of the actual joining,
and *Death,* we say. *Darkness-Beyond-Dreaming.*

A spirit old as rock sputters in me now, enraged
this poem will not sail to the sun, pierce the earth.
The daemon demands I listen more closely
to birdsong, the ghost-muttering of trees,
that I inhale the remains of words barely
there for want of attention—*flower head,*
bright-lit, besotted, wind-shorn—even as I lean
hard into the electric murmur short-circuiting
my synapses. Bleak signals turning the senses
to stone, incipient syllables in the blood to stuttering
current. Threatening to shut me up altogether.

The angel—whose quaint habit is skewed rhyme
and jazz-like syncopation, his range
a sunlit mountain at one end, black ocean
on the other—accepts no excuses. But we
can only stammer now. Syntax dislocated,
fractured, diary entries broadcast at the speed
of light. Desolation become like breathing
at sight of human flesh scattered as moldering
seed. Once fertile words, stacked like bodies
in the world's night, all we have to offer.

8

Holy the voices in the dark. Holy the hearer,
the one who refuses to hear, the one dying
and the one cradling the dying. Holy the altars—
even as they decay from lack of sound
and movement, praise and incantation,
longing and revolt—upon which you still lay
yourselves down. Holy what is gone,
what remains. Holy the world's night.

High Plains Book of the Dead

A Morality Play in One Act

The authentic voice of Western man
remains Job's…: petitioning, pleading,
deploring, damning, praying.

Sharon Doubiago

On the eve of his death,
a desperate man
asked God for mercy.

There was shuddering
in the aspen leaves, wind
so fragile a week-old child's

complaint could overwhelm it.
The man was suddenly mindful
of these facts, also of the moonlight,

turning his shadow regal
blue, and a solitary cricket's
canticle balanced against the erratic

beating of his heart, the song
overshadowing the snake of terror
writhing in his belly.

The trembling in the trees
became the trembling of the man
and he revoked his request.

He hummed a little with the cricket,
a seesaw up and down, felt
the snake in his stomach slough its skin

and become the sky, and he dreamt
he was once again a baby, sovereign
blue and cooing frantic syllables that,

like God, shimmered among the leaves,
sighed in the moonlight, echoed
in his shuddering, in these shadows turning—
                              this extravagant music.

Tending the Dead with Jazz Accompaniment

...six angels come over to hold up the folds of the
clouds and let water come down
just like a flood.

Norman Haskins

This rain refuses to lift until we again
achieve antediluvian certainty
the world is bird-bone hollow, empty
as a raindrop.

Until the trumpeted blues on the radio
enters our corpuscles and a dead man means
more than this inattentive stare and rot, until
his corpse gives up the ghost and sighs a truth

beyond mathematics in the fetid air above
a mattress no one will sleep on, fuck on,
daydream on again, that we'll burn when the clouds
dissolve and the sun is resurrected and the dead weight

of this man is hauled somewhere discrete,
his rigid beauty hidden from the light, filed
in the earth spacious enough to hold us all,
which will ring when he raps the backbeat, echo

like a night-filled glade when he whispers
the lyrics: a mist rising, a moan at the edge
of sleep asking us to remember, to know
beyond doubt, the world is bird-bone
hollow, empty as a raindrop.

Ode to the Insomniac

Something leaves you in the dark,
a piece of you better fettered to flesh
than floating about the world
as lonely feral exhalation. Not
your soul exactly, or spirit,
that diaphanous beast, but essential
nonetheless, you are certain. Awake
when all others are asleep, you realize
you are not lighter as such paring
away would seem to yield, but heavy
as if infused with molten iron. You
weep for grief you can neither measure
nor explain, for the loss of this portion
of you floating about the room,
then out the window to be dispersed
on the wind, never to return to its nest.
You are now no known animal, a thing apart
flying apart in the centrifugal force
of the turning earth. You pray
to the glowing clock for sleep, daylight
a thousand years away, and leak,
a fraction at a time, into the night.

The Man from Laramie

For George Grimm

This is the most unfriendly country I have ever been in…

James Stewart as Will Lockhart
in *The Man from Laramie*

Novels by Dostoevsky and Tolstoy
at your hip in lieu of loaded Colts, Rasputin's
unruly hair and black-flame beard flying, chest
out, shoulders forward, I see you forever
stepping smartly in night-black cowboy
boots down the sidewalks of this shit-heel town.

Like Bat Masterson strolled the dirt streets
of Abilene, Dodge City, Tombstone,
you are headed for another showdown
with evil in its atheist's ten-gallon hat.
A legend if ever one roamed
these small-town boulevards.

But it was grief killed you, a bullet
worthy of long-dead Russians who wrote
fat books as prayers to suffering: a woman,
your Anna Karenina but with poison-tipped
blades in her lace bodice, took your voice
and your will, left you a washed-up gunfighter
sleeping it off in a rented room.

Your last ride was on the big horse of dread
down a street named Sacrifice, named
Too Soon, named Forever. Petitioning Mary
as you lit out for the final territory, rosary
sliding through sawmill-mangled fingers,
slurred oaths from your bullet-riddled heart,
you bled like Jesus until empty.

A fellow outrider, the big man armed
only with poems and holed-up in the hinterlands,
a bounty on his head for being too honest, says
you ride through his dreams too. Calling
for your Anna in Jimmy Stuart's mellifluous

stutter as you pass the dives on Grand. Promising
protection, love, eternity... Anna never shows.

The outrider has renamed you Conscience,
even as you refuse to turn his way in dream
but spur your mount toward the border
where light ends utterly.

Taking a Walk

We say our road is dirt
but it is a geological
marvel. Schist and iron
and agate. Quartz mica-
flaked. Chert and knapped flint.

Our road flows, blended
eons lapping at our feet. Elemental
remains of hunters, fire tenders,
song masters, dust of great beasts
that roamed these plains before Adam
rising with our steps.

You coo as our children
might have years ago
and bend to pick up a pebble
striped like a sunfish, a stone
shaped like the head of Jesus
in a portrait from your grandmother's
house, a piece of heart quartz, blood-
lined, to keep in your sock drawer.

As we walk your pockets rattle
like a sacred gourd, a rhythm old as birdsong.
Nearby creek water a tongue in search
of a mouth, tumbling stones stuttering
clipped syllables. The dog stops
not far ahead, turns, and lowers her head
as if considering what manner of human—
stalkers of game, soothsayers, seekers
after forbidden knowledge—follow
her in the twilight.

Patron Saint

At the edge of a snow-battered northern
town where women bind their breasts
and men, their desire defying all constraint,
dream of bound breasts, a coyote lopes
toward the confluence of destiny and remorse.

The blue pickup swerves in the tempest,
a lost child saved. But this tale, repeated
in the Dead Dog Tavern for months after,
is still a tragedy. The man, too shaken to drive,
parks. Weeps. Curses his failures. Walks.

The storm now a beast even by cold-
country standards, he can see only his own
child's face in the white wall before him. Cherubic.
Terrified as the boy in the road for all the noise
of lives exploding. Then beckoning as if absolution
awaits in the colorless distance.

The world, night inverted, a grave inside out,
the land of penance stretches forever
from his grasp. The man stumbles, falls.
He does not attempt to rise but wraps himself
in white as if a sacrifice: the coyote, patron saint
of lost children in this cold land, will eat his eyes.

Elegy for Daylight

> *...suppose a rose to have sensation, it blooms on a beautiful morning it enjoys itself—*
> *but there comes a cold wind, a hot sun—it can not escape it, it cannot destroy its*
> *annoyances—they are as native to the world as itself: no more can man be happy in*
> *spite, the world[l]y elements will prey upon his nature. The common cognomen of this*
> *world among the misguided and superstitious is 'a vale of tears' from which we are to be*
> *redeemed... What a little circumscribed straightened notion! Call the world*
> *[instead]...the vale of soul-making.*
>
> John Keats

Daylight turned in upon itself, down
the long red tunnel to the involute heart
of the rose. It slept there, fetus-curled
but old beyond counting, dreaming
rebirth as a younger animal—
stealthy and proud and hunting.

Daylight also imaged its unfolding
as a fragile fist into a hand, a ruddy
palm turned skyward to expose
the terrible stigmata, the stunningly
beautiful wounds of everyday suffering.

But you and I, creatures of such hunger
we have longed to die with the dead, to have
them beyond the edge of breath
as we did not have them alive, dream

the slow breathing of the rose nightlong,
of daylight reincarnate in the rising blue
singing up and out the bloody throat.
Each day perhaps our last chance
to know another deep as soul-light.

Crazy Woman Canyon

On a river crooked as a man's ramble from broken love
to broken love, toward blood-ties sundered
and his bones buckled under the hooves of deer
a hundred years hence, tree swallows
skim the water, grace in the service of hunger.

The ghost of a madwoman wanders this canyon
afraid to stop singing lest her throat fill
with mayflies and silence. Her song, a miracle
of longing, stretches like fingers into dread. The sun
wanes among the scrub willow and pasque flowers,

and the trout I carry on a stripped twig stare
blank-eyed, the blue too strange to be home,
green-winged alien cousins swimming there, swooping
up from the margin between the mundane world
and the illusion of heaven. She invites me to lie here,

and I imagine the moon, already ascending, heedless
as it sails over and over and over the water... Coyotes
wail grace somewhere downriver, and the mad one,
alone in her grief for a century, picks up the chorus.
Her song of welcome rises from ten thousand gauzy

wings on her lips, a map to her in their striations,
instructions for how to love a ghost in the complex
rhythms of so many in the falling light. Rainbow
rise to peek at their dead kin as I turn toward
the canyon rim, the coyotes now focused
on their meal. The woman returns to her weeping.

Every Poem is a Love Song to Death

The space between words, the deep
caesura separating the penumbra of small
letter *l* from the double ax of capital *T,* for instance,
is the blank cartridge that divides a heartbeat
and a heartbeat, a momentary incarnation
of the void, nesting place of all silence.

Eternity also sleeps in the vastness
between voiced and unvoiced palatals, and between
the guttural hum of the *m* reclining and the forced march
of the *k*. You can almost see the letters shudder
with delight as one stutters to a close, exhausted,
to be answered across a universe of quiet
by the opening of the next, tiny flowers
of sound yielding to replacement that arrives
just in time to keep the garden blooming
another moment, then another.

                              We sing
to hold off the unassailable hush, but also
to become familiar with the grave-
light of the final period, the last
curl of the question mark that is a ringlet,
or perhaps a scar, on the forehead of God,
with the silence that stretches from this chair
where I decipher my own scrawl
to nowhere.

Commuter

For all its flashy eroticism, the commodity is an allegory of death.

Terry Eagleton

His toaster—sleek curves of steel that remind
him of a woman's ass, albeit with two crevices,
a female bottom forged by Picasso—beckons
this morning as if a siren offering manna.
A blood-red pastry or perhaps a bagel.
He pretends not to see the obliterating angel
smiling at him sideways from those twin slits.

His television—a palace of light stuffed with beautiful
corpses sprinkling the magic of attraction
over what he eats and drinks and wears and wants
beyond reason—before which he waits for his breakfast
predicts, with cleavage and a smile and slight pleasing lisp,
rain and a splash of sun for his commute.

His car—its sleek lines of animal-mechanical
grace, sufficient power to devour
not just miles but souls, his spirit-animal—
roars to life. Or so he dreams, shifting,
accelerating, behind the wheel. Power
that makes his cock quiver as he merges
with traffic. His womb, had he one, would tingle
with the need to bring forth life.

Or so he believes with certainty usually
reserved for death, taxes, and TGIF as the freeway
unfolds over a migration trail nearly as old as earth,
though he has no idea, over ground once forest-
covered, tangled in roots, breathing. No idea.
Then the taste of rot in his mouth as he exits
and boredom once again as if on cue. Turn right,
                    then left.
                              Park.

22

The Dog

A man shot a faded yellow cur,
scab-ridden nursery for fleas
and other beasts that sup
on the blood.

The man imagined the animal
lonely and in pain, limping
toward a meal of garbage,
toward a death no human dare envision.

But the dog was in fact the bearer
of a sacred thirst to roam
every alley on earth in search
of a prize poets have strained
thousands of years to name.

The vermin were her soul-mates,
the tiny devourers priests, revelators
of truths in small bites. The dog's broken
gait simply proof of rough passage,
of courage in the stale light of the world.

The dog felt the bullet enter behind
her left front leg, understood
without words to convey the news
that her lung was in tatters, the trail
of pissed-on walls and broken screen
doors and howling for joy in the night
to end right here.

The man stood over the tawny cur
as her breath turned liquid, then ceased,
not once seeing the absolute in the film
descending her eye, the chanting of the parasites
too faint to hear above the fearful roar
of his own heartbeat.

Animal Lessons

As it flees the body on split hooves
of vacancy and wind, an animal's
soul makes a noise so high and tight
heavenly beings shiver, birds scatter,
dogs stand on their hind legs and wail
like jazz musicians improvising
the end of the world.

The man who has heard this trans-
migrational clamor, part shriek,
part soughing in the leaves, lays
his head down every night thereafter
wiser and colder. He has heard,
just barely, his own soul quavering
in the same magnificent key, straining
to return to the wild. Upward. Out. Away.

Dreaming the Poetess

For Maggie Jaffe

In a place like the mind, switch-
blade precision and ocean vastness at once (*no,*
saturated with the terror of being), she balanced
on the precipice of a new kind of knowing
but could not budge for fear.

She felt like a fisherman on the void, her
line trailing through sweat and jism and heart-
wreck, through her foundering belief
in meaning, both hoping to hook and afraid
to hook the Leviathan rumored to swim
in the night-beyond-night.

Then it did not matter. The great beast-
fish burst from under where she sat
and gobbled her whole. No more prayers to light.
No tears for the turning earth that will spin
long after we all are thus swallowed, by grief
and the dawning horror that the impending
silence, soon to stretch from here to everywhere,
might be the sea of banality every poet fears.

No.

She said, *I possess only one word, no two words,*
and they are an excuse to go forward. I rub
them together to keep warm. No, to feel rich. No,
to feel something less than completely broke
and alone in this dimming interior. I shed
light like a star. I turn cartwheels. I sing
like a mermaid rides a wave, half
submerged and unafraid.

In a place glazed (*no, stained*) with the wonder
of being until that shimmer becomes the whole, the poetess
discovered a country beyond prayer. No,
beyond meaning itself, beyond deep-water silence

filled with the potential for music and provisional
sense born as sparks where two words meet. She said,

Hold these words to you gently but hard as iron. Say
them over and over. Love and decay. No, emptiness
and truth. No, time and blood. No and yes.
The infinite (sacred) land between.

Dirt and Something Divine

He spent the last year of his life
chanting the name of God, survived
on canned tuna and turnips from his garden,
whiskey that made his ulcers bleed.

He named his ulcers as if constellations,
recited poetry in every language
but his own, refused to speak in the dark.
Practice, he said.

He would not eat except at dawn
when light is just being born.
The dream of hope, he said. He drank
to the moon but offered no explanation.

He spent the last year of his life
trying to forget all the women
he ever knew. He warned
them loudly he could not be sorry.

That last summer, his roses
bloomed as if forever is a petal
within petals. The rains came
and went. He chanted and blew

kisses to the old woman
next door, slept on the porch
in an old man's chair, told jokes
in his dreams. The God of his childhood,

surrounded by women in silk so fine
their flesh shimmered through,
laughed. The man chanted even
as the women sang their refusal
to apologize. He blew them kisses anyway.

He chanted the name of God
and the women in his dreams carried
him through the dark, weighted

his eyelids with rose petals, gave
him a final kiss that tasted of dirt
and something, he understood only just then,
divine.

As in a Fairytale…

—a curse on the land, a fallen prince—darkness bends around every object, each actor straining for a moment mistaken for culmination, the moral of recent circumstances that nearly killed them. Though they barely realize it. Some summary judgment, a moral, that allows sufficient solace to forget, if only for a moment, the shapeless beast lying in wait beyond the edge of the black forest.

At a sidewalk café I follow my breath, anchor and pneumonic, on the fourth day of a depression spawned, per usual, of the ordinary. Deepened just now by report of a famous stranger's death. As laborers from the road repair down the block sip coffee and wait for their lunch, a man in red shirt and midnight-blue tie slaps down the joker, the hanged man, the death card. Tragedy with rim shot. A woman wearing a silver crucifix, her fingers nimble as mice, pantomimes the cross.

She says, "This happens in threes. Did you hear about…" I brace for more news to withstand one dull-blade syllable at a time, another man's noose punching me in the esophagus. To tongues clicking the beat of dismay, I consider the missing integer, the absent third term, the as-yet-to-come proof.

The condemned, whose brain conspires to end him, accepts the impossibility of reprieve, wolves at the door and any house with his name on the mailbox made of straw. Knows any snippet of glib conversation could be the last he has to endure even as he kicks like a dog running in dream at the air threatening to crush him.

The man in the red shirt draws the lovers card, the wheel of fortune, the strength card. "There must have been a woman," he says, "too much faith in the inane, a terminal case of bad humor—ironic for a professional funny man—because of the downturned market…"

I imagine the dead man's T-bone cooked just right, a night-black stout followed by sex with his beloved under starlight as Little Walter wails on a harmonica forged by the gods. Phone calls from his grown children he wishes he could have made into something to wear over his heart as he stares out his rich man's window at the perfect lawn, beds of zinnias, pool reflecting moonlight. *No matter. No matter. No matter.*

Every day is colored a menacing shade, blood at the edges. Every sunrise another battle, each sunset only provisionally won. *Not today, but…* Then, one ordinary Sunday, the creature just beyond his peripheral vision whispers of worthlessness, of rest, his belt over a closet door as portal.

No more staring into his cup waiting for this fit to pass. No more tearing at his clothes among faux shamans and gossips, hungry workmen, lovers sharing a laugh amidst the tinkling of spoons in cheap ceramic cups. The blue sky exhorting them, sustaining them. The green earth too.

Among nonchalant bystanders who swear "It happens in threes…," he ponders the gravity of such bleak numerology, ponders inevitable rumors of jealous queens and poisoned apples. Synapses short-circuited to ash, he turns toward the darkling wood. The well-trod path in.

High Plains Book of the Dead
For Shell

The coyote sprawls next to the blacktop,
legs extended before him,
or so it looks from here, tongue
slack on the October air and dripping.
I slow to look closer. *Sick? Car struck?*

His legs are cut off at the joint, clean
as if by a surgeon. No blood. Just blue-white
rings of bone like the circles of a lopped tree.
Gangrene or starvation: hell in the next roll
of the dice no matter which side up.

Should they be robbed of their last moments,
the agonized glide from fragmented sunlight
into the wholeness of dark, their pain
the epitome of being, a chaos they desire
even as they wish to escape it, do the suffering
forgive us if we lose the capacity to speak what we see?

The coyote rises on the stumps of his front legs
as I reach behind the seat for an ax, hobbles
up the knoll and turns at the fence line
as if beckoning me to follow with the blade.

The barbed wire pricks my finger, blood
spreading over the ash handle, the honed
steel head. I survey prairie stretching
to the horizon, empty as the hand that cannot hold
a tool, a pen, a lover firmly enough for fear
all creation will float away. The coyote gone.

*

Unable to speak in your passion, sister,
you motion for help, a magician casting
a spell that threatens to split me to atoms. I help
you turn to your left side, your hands

in my hands, a minimalist promenade
before settling you gently to the bed.

Three heartbeats later you motion again.
I turn you, feather light, planet heavy,
to your back, and place your head gently
as breath on the pillow. Your hands
flutter above you in a pantomime of birds,
and I turn you to the right. Our pas de deux
ending, at last, in sleep, your every third breath
stalls a full half minute for the next twenty.

Awakening with a start, your voice
returned as a bird to the nest, you ask me
to hold your head in my hands, your hair
like water I know must eventually escape
through my fingers. *Get that goat a can,*
you say. *No, that was a long time ago.*
But I hurt someone just now, you tell me,
a dream leaking into your bedroom.
I will do better next time. Better.

You say, *Do a funny dance.* Though all
those steps seem funny now, I left my moves
somewhere in 1979. You repeat, *1979.*
Me too. Whose dog is that howling?
I don't hear anything. *Probably the wild
dog I saw limping a while ago, running
sideways like he was magic. But wounded.
He was so wounded. Tumors sharp as knives.*
Put that in a poem, you say. *Tumor-sharp.*

Then a moan. Part question. Part the sound
of surprise. *I wanted to name that wild dog,
but he already has a name. A name
I don't remember.* Your hands flutter
upward again, frantic birds rising
into the air. I move you to the left, a gentle
lift and placement. Then to the right.
Every particle of me threatens to fly apart.

*

For forty nights the coyote ambles awkward
through my dreams, a mutilated breeze
on bloodless half-legs. Some nights
he stops to stare at me, fur glistening
in the half-light of the high plains in fall. Outraged,
I assume, by the inadequacy of the witness.

I wake and step to the window to stare
into the black. Sirius first loping, then
stumbling through the sky, then lying
down as if never again to rise.

Noir Love Song

A Friend in Midlife

Your night dreams of stagnant
water, daydreams of flight,
you declare angels a vicious
joke bequeathed by our ancestors
laughing at us from beyond
the stars, love a distasteful myth
perpetuated by villains.

You tell me and the bartender—a tattoo
over her right breast of Bosch's bird-headed
monster eating and shitting humans—
you no longer ache for what you can't name,
no longer believe in the benevolent arc
of chance. Possibility a young woman
with a twinkle in her eye, mere provocation
to prove us fools.

Your days are numbered, you say—
as the bartender moves on to other
forlorn tales—and as in a fixed carnival
trick you know the balance. Death
all but crossed the i's and dotted the t's.
And when you stand still, you say loudly
as if trying to get someone's attention,
you hear rusty leaves aswirl in your heartbeat
and so slouch like a corpse to get used to the posture.

How can I answer? Shadows
hovering near the door—an old man
drunkenly singing a tune unheard
for decades (*a wayward bloke*
on a wayward trek stumbles
when he hears his childhood name…),
two women with eyes downcast,
whispering, his muses either plotting
or merely distraught—are surely a sign
just for you. The road ahead gets darker.
Brace yourself. Remember how to sing.

Noir Love Song

A scaffold of tangled jazz
bridges the quiet at the sharp
edge of conversation, your
newly professed enemy
running her thumb down
that blade as she stares
at the soft skin of your throat.

Then Miles plumbs the depth
of the blues in a dangerous key,
the residual resonance of joy
warping down its tawny length
to become a single violent note
you hold to the light to map

its fissures, the chasms and dark
timbre where wolves circle. You want
to look away, to tell her a bloody tale
to match Miles' atonal bellow. You want
to riff on a duet of sacrifice and naked
détente you once knew by heart.

But the song ends and the horn player
steps into shadow for a moment. Like
Berryman before Shakespeare, tears
in honor of the varied terrain of creation,
the untoward key changes, the improvisations
and sidewinder rhythm, a bluesman's cryptic grief.

The next tune begins in a squalor
of C sharps and she is again triple-tonguing
incantations on the air, spells of unbinding.
You hum along in monotone, the vacant
noise of fields aflame and houses smoldering,
of the very stars convulsing. The single
threadbare note of any terrible conflagration.

Dead People Hate the Number Two...
Garcia Lorca

Entangled. Motionless except
for the tiny harmonic flutter
playing along the curve of our ribs
where we intersect. Alone
except for the jealous dead
wishing for hands to explore
another's face, lips to suckle,
voices to speak the ten thousand
notes of flesh they shed
to become utter vacancy.

Our single shadow moves up the wall
in the faltering sunlight, puddles
near the ceiling a few moments
before fading to black. Shared
sweat-shimmer and mixed perfume of us
the saddest measures of the lost earth,
perhaps ghosts find some peace
doing our simple math in reverse.

Tableau: Hawk and Lovers

The hawk an arc in the plane geometry
of light, a nodal point of reference—
to itself and to heaven—from which the sky
extends forever in the imagination.

The hawk a battlefield transformed
by wind and a bewildering desire
to sail on before your words
dissolve under scrutiny.

The hawk a heartbeat defying the order
to stop, a spark in the embers, destiny
by another name, sacred and terrible
to behold. Remorseless, the talons.

The hawk an angel not quite stillborn
in the darkest age of the world, born to ride
the enormity of consciousness, of the earth
spinning, the poem that goes on forever.

The hawk rides the thermals over
the Wyoming prairie, a thought
and a flesh and blood gift, the dream
of a god with a feathered heart.

The hawk in the sky. The hawk
in your voice as you drift
away toward another life, another
light, as you soar toward a new home.

The hawk a harbinger of our fate,
I kiss you to sleep, the wind
rising, the year turning, the last
light of the world gone so low.

Crepuscular Velvet: B's California Story

> *The name hidden in its potency possesses a power of manifestation and*
> *occultation, of revelation and encrypting. What does it hide? Precisely the abyss*
> *that is enclosed within it. To open a name is to find in it not something but*
> *rather something like an abyss, the abyss as the thing in itself.*
> Jacques Derrida

He said he had his doubts in an alley
that could have been L.A.
except it was San Bernardino
where lost seagulls shit on his car
and no one is an aspiring actress.

Not this woman with a stage name
on her knees by a dumpster, this woman
who told him her sister makes commercials
in Hollywood but spends time genuflecting
for money too. The familial craft, he wondered?
In the bar she claimed to be 22, but by afternoon
alley light looked old enough to be her own mother.

The distant traffic swelled as she explained
her name and unzipped his pants: *the fresco*
of night coming on in the desert, the voluptuous
touch of the air. Then she sighed—so dramatically,
he said, Garbo would have blushed, so filled
with untranscribable meaning that a dull ache
climbed deep into his spleen—then she began
and he never knew what hit him. What buxom
sadness as desire descended like a thousand
pound overcoat made of, yes, crepuscular velvet.

Truth or Dare: The Movie Trailer

A blonde in wrap-around sunglasses
and red spike heels, her dress bleak
blue, dares our hero, as in an adolescent
game, to tell her a truth. Any truth. Bleeding
is not sufficient prelude to deeper meaning,
she says, as buzzards circle out the window,
to even a minor epiphany, let alone love.

The hero stares at the patterns in her expressionist
wallpaper, all moody angles and failed poetic
devices, as she tends the bullet hole in his stomach,
stares at her tattooed flesh become part
of the scenery: her three lost children, a dog
named Falstaff, a beauty in bleak blue
stapled to a tree like Jesus.

John Lee Hooker sings in the background
as scenes of war flicker in the next room. Jungle-
gore from their childhoods rebroadcast in the harsher
light of the desert. Shakespeare's bloody stage
ten thousand shifting pixels and explosions
in surround-sound.

She shows him her breasts in grim kitchen
light, small and proud. A gift reserved
for heroes like you, she says. He tells
her he can't stay except long enough to kiss,
first the right, then the left, then in between
where her perfume burns his tongue. The fire
falling from the sky in the next room
a portent we fail, as always, to recognize.

The Constellation of Remorse

Dread is a woman in high heels,
her offset nipples staring accusations
that joy would die in my house,
her smile a lie I would kill to believe.

I want to ask her to dance
but the bartender is her brother
and certain I stink of poverty,
the worst crime in America.

My table wobbles like an old man
on ice. The chair leans as a funhouse
trick. The jukebox plays only Hank
Williams and the air smells of sex and ruin.

A sly man would leave before he can no longer
hear the music over the basso din of his blood,
before the dancer turns away, her breasts

a glimmer of heaven in the mind, before
the bouncer asks to see my money.
A cunning man would find the back door
and step out under the stars

in an ally so piss-soaked feral cats
avoid it. A shrewd man would look up
to chart his course home and never speak
of love or salvation again in this life.

Noir Snapshots

He called at midnight from a payphone,
artifact of an earlier civilization, to ask
forgiveness for his sins, real and fabricated.
The ringing incessant, cloying.
The anti-music of his dreams.

The receiver reminded him of her. Hard
to the touch, heavy of thought, her merciless
buzzing in a minor register. He left the phone
dangling, teal plastic swinging in artificial light,
bouncing off the spit-stained glass suffused with wire.
A broken metronome winding down.

He imagined the ringing received
in a far galaxy millennia hence, a message
the brightest alien minds can't decipher.
The monotone certainly meaningful,
they will say. Perhaps the wavelength
of the sender's thoughts. Stuttering rhythm
of circulating corporeal fluids.
Call sign of distress.

From his seat at the scarred linoleum counter
in a ruined truck stop off the interstate,
he wishes for better coffee, wishes his angry
waitress beautiful and kind. Wishes his children
peaceful sleep, lives filled with riches and love.
He wishes for a message from a far star system
he might ponder unto his last breath, for an omen
of better fortune in a piece of cardboard pie.

For an Ex

The last hours—of a day, marriage,
life—are sacred. We should speak
those hours as prayer, count them down
to the last, to zero, and perhaps appreciate
the hand of cosmic irony at work: eternity,
as in to-have-and-to-hold, divided by nothing.
Instead, I bow to the western horizon
and fend off fantasies of a different ending.

A meadowlark sings for a mate from barbed
wire, his heart keeping the beat at 200 per minute,
every *thrum* a distinct chord, or so I imagine,
as the bird hits the right note every time, each
a perfect song unto itself.

I manage to hum Blind Willie McTell
as the sun goes down (*you made me
hug you and you made me cry*), resolve
to speak poetry in the name of everyone
I have ever loved. And losing my tenuous
hold on birdsong, which slips toward the darkness,
I imagine an end without cold streets, holes
in the soles of my shoes, our bed sheets
carnage-stained, curse-riddled, split.

I count backward to zero
imagining the numerals above
a childhood school-room blackboard,
your fingernails on slate, scratching
away at all my words.

The Sorrows
For Tu Fu and Gerald

A certain woman's winter-white thighs
turning in sunlight, her voice a bugle of discontent.
Aged whiskey spilled from a cut-glass tumbler
to stain a rabbit's foot bequeathed by an alcoholic poet
with a broken lung and less luck than the rabbit...

Memory rides the sky like a delinquent bird
of ill omen, blood on its talons, carrion-
stained beak—cruel clouds forming
these patterns before the moon.

History

Try to praise the mutilated world…
Adam Zagajewski

History rides lines of type
like a returning train. Death
in a bomb vest. Kidnapped girls
sold to finance a war. Drone-strike
collateral and stray bullets scattered
among sugar-sweet lies that always
lead to rubble for our enemies, burning
clothes, ribbons of flayed skin.

I wad the news, place it
in a rock hearth beneath a pine,
heap dry needles, twigs,
and set the pile alight. Crossed
sticks catch. Ash, sparks drift
upward, the wind pulling
it all apart a word at a time.

I made love to my first wife
on this ledge of crumbling
granite more than thirty years
ago. Biafrans starving down
her ice white thighs. A million
Cambodians tortured behind
her ribcage. Dire forecast of a dirty
bomb at her lips to one day blow
the marriage asunder.

The sky gray that day, this flame
arrived three decades late. Smoke
and cinder on the breeze move
the mind beyond that mutilated
image—beyond the last words,
last rites, and endless return
of suffering—to two red tail hawks
on the breeze. For a moment,

king and queen of the air, then gliding
over the bloody rim of the known world.
                            Gone.

Sacred Ground
for Sharon

Your wrists are maps to an inviolate land,
charts of rivers from which no man
has sipped, into which no woman has dipped
her finger for the slightest taste.

The door of daylight also opens precisely
there, at the confluence of your hand
and arm you dream feathered, the better
to take you to another world where, circled
by a yet sweeter light, you have told me,
you will never again need to sleep.

Then this more mundane revelation
as I rise to make my way to the bath:
desire can be roused by something
so simple as sunlight falling along a wrist,
the sacred land between a river and a wing.

Lessons

First Lesson

Under Nebraska sky—the blue hand of God
that is also the map of eternity—the boy
hunkers under a cottonwood that will outlive him
studying a nakedness too desperate to touch.
The beast's tiny yawn threatens to tear the world—heroic
tales of trails through wilderness, settlements
birthed along the way with named water towers, owls
calling comfort outside his window in the night—asunder.

Upon a cracked sidewalk—soon a perilous river
rolling toward lands under meaningless clouds
where he will one day stumble, compassless
and alone, remembering this animal as he contemplates
his father's corpse cooling on a steel table—the boy
stares as in dream at the feeble monster tottering forward,
slipping to the ground, rising, mad to assay cornfields
and towns from the simmering air as its blood promises.
The child does not see a single sign of fur or down,
and his only thought after fear fades: is this creature cold?

Another boy, older, squats then too, identifies
this sightless misery as *a bird lost*, its home
a rumor among the high branches, explains
that its mother cannot—or maybe he said *will not*—
retrieve it. The smaller boy shakes his fist at heaven,
a tiny Elijah demanding this unimaginable sin
be reversed, the map of the bird's world be redrawn
to include a bright place called *Shelter,* called *Love.*

The older boy palm-cradles the bird
as it squawks rage at the negligent god of flight,
slips it into his breast pocket and climbs. But not far.
The tree too big. Branches leagues apart.
He places the robin on a limb high as he can reach
as he hollers lies of solace to the younger child—
she will surely find him here—who, like the man
remembering, weeps for the fallen, for the wreck
of the world, all maps gone gray, all lands labeled Death.

Rhubarb

By summer's hard light
rhubarb holds green like
a boy carries hope.
But a red and white
stucco house haunts him,
a woman gasping
on cold linoleum
like a fish, saying
over and over she
can't forgive the man
in his shiny blue suit
and scuffed shoes. His
whiskey breath. Failed
Lancelot. Failed Jesus.
His father the savage
avatar of a gospel
she cannot stomach.

Years after the fish
on the floor, her bloody
oaths, the boy hangs
a shotgun-killed hawk
on barbed wire, his family
crest and coat of arms.
Visions of life-long
knighthood in service
to a lead-cold queen who
hates him, he wheels away
from this heraldry
and would hurry home,
veering left at the wild
patch of rhubarb, searing
green stunning him
to greater speed, if he
believed in the possibility.

The Hermit's Promise
For Gerald

From the sunlit side of a frozen pond
he stares skyward. Winter clouds, shattering,
let just enough warmth through to make him smile.
I lean into the wind at his side, unsure
how to survive when he disappears, this magician,
killer of demons threatening to take up residence in my skull.
But I already wrote that poem, his busted lung
run through by the endless shiv of an empty highway.

He says, wheezing upward, he will not let me down.
This fallen poet in long-handled drawers swears
to hold them accountable, those who slid a knife
between my ribs, betrayed me with a kiss, lied to
and stole from and grieved me. He'll conjure
them all on my behalf, shout curses to the night,
toast the villains' demise with whiskey distilled
from their pecker-head souls...

But, he says, I must promise too: more poems
and other, less elegant, diatribes on *his* behalf,
a toast to the half-clad moon as Motown plays
in the background, Sam and Dave or Delta
blues he suggests I might also sing at his funeral.
The only one there. His apprentice. But no tears,
no tears, no tears, he insists. Just a salute
to winter sky. To shattered light.
The brotherhood thereof.

Depression Poem

The angel's voice, a song played
on a comb covered in wax paper,
buzzes transcendence like a threat.

The angel is bedraggled, for only
such a creature can be so savagely divine,
skinny arms like ghosts on the wind.

I wrestle him daily, the creature
whose grip is python-strangle, whose
name I don't dare speak lest I burst

into flame. I hold the angel down,
wrap my legs around his, slap
his face, dislodge a tooth.

But he is stronger, every day, cuffs
me breathless between my shoulders,
pokes me in the eye. Moe to my Curley.

I roll to my back, lift a leg to signal
surrender, omega to his alpha, and close
my eyes against his triumphant laugh.
An irony so bleak even I should be amused.

Then I go about my life, the angel
of torture beating out-of-kilter time
on my forebrain, humming the soundtrack.
Same jaundiced tune. Another day.

What Direction Home?

Orpheus to Hermes in the moldering
dark below ground. Oedipus to his child
in the self-inflicted dark above. Rilke,
blinded by light, to his angel. Written
on a bar napkin and hung above the TV
for drunks to ponder between innings.

I imagine a map, dictated by spirits
and too complex to follow, and wandering
in circles like the rest. I ask the stranger
next to me where I am, how to get out. Her eyes
go dreamy as she delivers the lie, pretending
like all of us to know each turn, every street,
which door we can enter without knocking.

Allegory of a Metaphor

He always carried his own water,
almost since he could walk,
the wind so fierce in his face
it threatened to halt each stride.

              Early on the bucket
sprung a leak. His shoes grew wet,
then soaked and sloshing as he trudged,
but the pail was always full, heavy
as a heart atrophying, a life turned
leaden, a millstone, anchor, granite
grave marker.

              Memories, he says, made him,
first, too sluggish to fly, then pushed him further
into the earth with every step. Now, when he drinks
he repeats for strangers the opening words
to a single prayer: *I always carried my own water,*
almost since I could walk, up this damned hill.

Looking for Mercy: A Rough Blues

I flipped a coin, knocked
wood, stood on one foot
and held my index finger
in the air to determine
the direction to flee.

I hailed cleverness
by name, shook my fist
at split-hooved evil
as it sprinted toward me,
tasted the salt blood of a virgin,
and still the rain fell.

I dreamt the universe
made of threes, counted steps,
played my muse with her tulip
lips and spring-taut thighs
for a fool—she was my betrayer.

I saw the future in the shape
of a cloud but held my tongue,
hoping to die before the devil
woke again and found me stumbling
down the road alone.

I walked all the way to Kansas,
turned around and hitchhiked
to the sea with a woman of enormous
courtesy. I pled innocent
but failed to hold my mouth just right.

Mercy would not show herself,
would not untie me and wish me well,
would not show me the secret map
she carries, folded neatly, in her pocket.

Mercy has since sent word
she's forgotten even my name, the road

to my door, but not the smell of me sweating
bullets. Mercy whose heart is steel, her soul
pea-sized, her eyes a stranger's wishing me dead.

The Contrivances
For G.

A good two-dollar watch. T-bone
with a side of beans. Trout
of sufficient quantity and size
to make a story. A woman,
named for a bird or a flower,
wearing Harley chaps
with the ass cut out. Contrivances
we lay end to end to save our lives
like a bridge over an abyss.

         But sometimes
only a rope, thin and frayed. Old
Crow from the bottle, paid-for sex
with a woman who cannot stop crying,
bologna on store-bought rye, and nary a bite
where the god of trout himself once swam.

            Sometimes, a dream
       of thin air stretching at our feet
            as far as the eye can see, the hollow
             sound of wind through our ribs, heartbeat
               all tatters, fragments, and nowhere to go
   but down.

Surfaces...

The thinness of contemporary life. I could
put my finger through it.

Don DeLillo

the glittering, the bloody, the inane, reflecting
off other surfaces endlessly as if Indra's
jeweled net but without thunder, exchange
of fluids, any words more profound than a jingle.
The sheen diffused until silicon-wafer thin.
The chaotic sea of images a quark deep. A sigh.
Something once called a chortle with just a touch
of irony. But never anything cosmic, that forgotten
art or joke. No one remembers which.

I want to put my index finger through this modern life
just to hear the tiny pop of nothingness. Poke holes
to reveal the darkness, the silence that came before
the ceaseless car horns and explosions and basso denials
of responsibility in the few remaining dialects, before trillions
of desolate public conversations, massacres brought to you
by Chevy and Exxon and Johnson and Johnson, punks
at the podium pretending to understand—truth itself
a cosmic irony if we still recognized it.

Poke holes to reveal the silence and darkness before a random bolt
through sludge. Before paramecia dancing spastically, trumpeting frogs,
yodeling birds, apes gamboling in twilight. Before hooves over tundra.
Rhythm. Before men and women moaning agony and orgasm.
And Blues. Before John Lee Hooker and Bach and the thunder
of skin drums, feet pounding dust. Before the tiniest glimmer
of a poem. Before we pulled it all thin as sheerest gauze.
The bloody. The glimmering. I want to poke holes
in this contemporary life as an act of faith.

Lonely Dancer

O ever more escaping grasp of things... Rilke

Every line begins with *I*, ends with *I*.
The closing punctuation an exclamation point,
ghost of an *I* shouting the world down
out the slim slit of itself to hold the 10,000
things at bay as if with virtual barbed wire.

The world is not "too much with us now"
so much as near utter absence, the self
a lonely dancer in bleak space. No birdsong.
No taint of rot. No scent of lilac but as virtual
symbol of something (also) missing.

No war dead mumbling ghost complaints. No
painted dancers enacting the final moments of the day.
No moon rising. No signs of a mind clawing its way
to remembrance, scratching toward forgetting. No
lover except as trope for the merest trace of longing or disdain.

This tattered chair. The Steller's jay out the window.
That woman's beauty mark. All completely lost
any moment now. This I-filled book in my hand fading
to wavelength and a stutter of current. That dog's
howl a transmission bounced off a satellite.

We hunger for something of heft. A five-pound
telephone receiver as in a Bogey movie to carry
the weight of real news. About wind and snow,
the next war, who is dying of what. A roll of coins
that are potential. For bread, a ticket out, a lover's keepsake.

A piece of blood quartz to commemorate a friend's
passing. Heavy in the hand, the pocket, the heart.
A lug wrench that rings on pavement. A cracked cup
from which someone's grandfather once drank. Steel pan
for bread. Iron skillet for potatoes and trout.

We long for a wrought thing. An arrowhead, sculpture

of some aspect of God, baseball hand-stitched. A well-turned
phrase from any mouth, symphonic in its implications.
A hood ornament like a carving of Persephone on the bow
of a ship to hell. This ghost ship empty of things wrought, things

with heft to hold flesh to bone and perhaps calm the erratic
waves in our skittish brains long enough to again love this life,
to have a real thought. *I*, says the poet who should give us the world,
and *I*, and in between are random finger taps and a ghostly thumb
on the electronic scale, any residual residue of earth red-shifting
toward the silence after a shouted end-stop.

A Man's Life
For Eli and Jesse

Lightning hit him when he was looking
the other way, in the direction
of the last fist of violent light
to punch him between the shoulder
blades and nearly stop his heart.

He curses at the clouds, declares
God a bully, tells the universe made
of such unjustness to screw itself,
to rear back and throw another bolt
if it has the balls. And of course it does,
big and brass. And it will, white hot
and perfectly aimed.

But that is a worry for another day.
The man tends his wounds, brushes
the ashes from his singed clothes,
and puts one foot in front of the other
down the road he has chosen. Again whistling
a tune of invincibility as a new storm
to the west rumbles its threat to burn
him to a crisp.

This is all he knows:
how to go forward, unafraid
of the next flash and boom
even as the smell of burnt ozone
                              still hangs in the air.

Why Write?

Another day, perched on your porch
among columbine, asters, peonies,
the petit bourgeoisie, pondering
your neighbor's baroque coiffure.
Which in turn leads us to consider
the sublime. The noble, the splendid,
the terrifying. In nature and the attempt
in art. In the curve of cloudless blue
over that bonnet of hair, perfect
as if chiseled from stone, as she plucks
weeds from her rose bed. Or perhaps
sprouted there as one more blossom.
Or exuded as a halo, aura of keratin
and volatile chemicals sprayed from a can
to keep her handiwork from dissipating
on the wind. A masterwork of wave and nuance,
of living cells gesturing toward death.

We agree—a rare enough event a meadow lark
offers a musical amen—that amidst their daffodils
and begonias, the unreconstructed inheritors
of toxic lawns and an old-fashioned angst
so profound they count it a second spleen,
another lung, the message is clear. Be calm
in the face of inevitable decline, brave
when the flowers fail, joyous even
as bolts of gray foretell final collapse.
Create something to challenge the sky.

Poet in (Perpetual) Wartime

Virgil on Main Street: Bone-White

For Leonard, who told me he feared becoming thus...

Not man, though man I once was... Dante

This night—a burial cloth
for the waning deeds of men,
the smell of Hell tarnishing the air
as in Dante's dream—reeks
of moldering souls stranded
between setting sun and waning moon.

I carry a bottle wrapped in a paper bag
and swear at traffic as if passing cars
carried men and women who might
understand, recognize this warning,
take it deep as a kiss that blossoms
to raging need, and *act*. A word
no longer kept warm and humming
in any dictionary, no longer the companion
of *passion* or even *desperation*. Only of *war*.
Perhaps the last enigma: the crumbling to dust
of everything with nary a hand lifted in protest.

Bone-white is an abstraction
until you see thousands of 700 year-old skulls
stacked neatly in a church on the plains
of Eastern Europe, the plague-dead
gaping, a choir of virulent silence
for the one true king, vagabond
ruler of empty eye sockets and broken
teeth and occipital divisions like a map
to the invisible country, the crazy line
of a river to nowhere multiplied
by these myriad. The many war dead
now a bone-white mountain
I must climb in my dreams.

The rough tenor of impending death
sounds in a truck's horn, the driver

annoyed by my gamboling in the intersection,
my poet's rancor that my words have forked
no lightning, the world no less bloody
for all my ranting. I try to forgive
the driver, for fallen angels
are frightened by their mortality
and imagine killing anything reeking
of vigor. One-eyed poets especially.

The fallen pretend none of it is happening:
the blithe dead smiling from fresh piles
on the nightly news, the mass graves,
the skulls on the altar, the twin chandeliers
made of femurs and lumbar vertebrae
over a general's snow-white baby grand.
The truck's horn screams again.

Imagine a fistful of iambs like a thrown bottle
in its brown skirt. Imagine syllables shattering
on sheet metal. Imagine lightning as if words
mattered. But only the driver, now more afraid
for his life than daily, fills my vision, his face
flame red and eyes wide with terror as if he too
just glimpsed the future.

Virgil on Main Street: Of Memory

The universe is a carbon copy
of the mind: light and dark
in a chaos of steps, forward,
back and around, a pas de deux
of being and its precursor,
a grand hurtling through time
beautifully fractured.

But this is not what I want
to tell you. A woman
steps to the corner in high
heels, her broken reflection
like diamonds on the wet
road at her feet, shattered
glass green and fire-truck red,
the shine on the street a Jackson
Pollack orgasm as perception splits
and splits again, forming and reforming,
rising up her stout legs, riding
her belly like her dream of a child,
standing up her throat like shouted song
to become chemistry in her brain,
to whistle in her blood with the wind.

And this is the beginning of the world,
dirty-perfect, a frameless picture sans
our spastic weeping for all that we desire
and cannot have, all that slips
through the senses and into the mind
only to decay an instant later.

The woman in red limps across
the broken glass to enter the sea,
to be carried away on the riptide of memory,
to sink deep. But one day in the rain
she will rise again to stand on a corner,
surprised by my ancient poet's face,
the sudden spew of gems at her feet.

Virgil on Main Street: Grief's Roots
For L.M. and E.B.

Three crows, living jewels riding
the white air, an inversion
of the flames they portend, descend

to become three carrion angels hung
in the limp heart of a late-winter tree, an ominous
convocation to witness the sky hump the earth,

the earth too tired in March to push back,
bleeding black from every orifice. Her
pelvic curvature sinks near the tree,

an infant skull pushing through the surface
to say nothing in a thousand dialects. No
prayer. No complaint. No cry for comfort.

No warning of what will inevitably come.
The dreamt earth's screech of strangled
syllables, frost pushing stones against bone,

stuns me awake. Then wind
in the eaves and shrill hum of night,
grief's roots generations deep.

American Fairytale

It was his oft-repeated history:
a bullet through the neck
while wearing a noose,
but his kerchief another man's
blood. The story went on
like this, one gore-stained
detail after another. But more
was said in the deep pause
between words, the hum
of the syllables after his lips
stopped moving: it was war
and he fell in love, then a child
with his blue eyes, another
in his sights who reminded him
of no one in that moment.
Night terrors all these years later.
Children waltzing through his sleep.
One with blue eyes.
One with no eyes at all.

The One-Armed Man Sings

For the depressed young vet at the grocery…

The reflection that he must someday be taken apart like an engine or a clock…and worked up into arches and pyramids and hideous frescoes, did not distress this monk in the least.

Mark Twain,
Innocents Abroad

My hand, gone ahead to reconnoiter
the darkness, makes the sign for man,
for the silence of the masses, the power
of the thousand things that sit on my heart
like lead but weigh no more than smoke
rising from a corpse. Makes the sign for peace
in an age of sun-hot shrapnel and machetes
and bomb-laden drones like volatile angels
overhead. My hand directs the sonata
in G-sharp for continents moving, the groaning
earth, the song of decay. My sundered fingers
run the rosary of pebbles and worms, rot
and sins no god with a conscience could forgive.
My arm—next to the arm with the scythe,
the arm holding the scales—waves to the crowd
whispering down there, to the rumored light above,
then gestures to the rest of me wandering
these aisles of cans and boxes, as if lost
in a sacred crypt made of the willing
bones of more prayerful men, in search
of some relief. My arm, my hand beckoning.

Poet and Bomb

The soul split like a melon
by the concussive vibration
of the air. Revised

and split again. Halves
to quarters to ad infinitum.
Molecules of flesh vaporized

to become the vibrating
air itself. Death-
shimmer on the wind

a kind of weather
to make us weep, our
hearts stutter as if hearing a great poem.

The poet had been speaking
just a moment before,
his tongue dancing along his teeth

deft as a dagger to cut
the undifferentiated whole
into swaths of created marvel.

The truth in a single Hebraic preposition.
Universe in the Arabic verb. Persian
nouns trotting double-time. Until

a frightened man blew him sideways
into silence. Until his tongue
wafted on the air it previously sliced.

A last divine exhalation
and all song became this single
hummed note: the ringing in our ears
that overwhelms every word.

A Passing Taxi's Radio...

plays a tune like viper slither,
like a financier laughing,
a tank turret turning.

Then silence as at the center
of a stone. The exile barely
falters and the world shifts.

Scuffing his toe against a curb,
his mind catches on a nail of regret
as if through his wrists, feet, heart.

The rubble of a collapsed city
all he can remember. Grackles
coughing. Wind. Dust.

Flowers have faded from human
memory. Hate is an organ,
more lung than appendix.

Tongues, turned to ash, complain
all around him. His fault. His sins
come home to roost on wings of soot.

The dead are here somewhere, lying
in ambush. He wonders how they know
him, his uniform burned long ago.

Then he is back. The curb
but a tiny cliff surrounded
by footsteps and horns blaring.

But the tongues still wag, whisper
of ash, of nails driven with a stone.
An insurgent cloud staining the sun.

Just Like Berlin
For Mr. H.

A man gray as dead bark
praises the sunrise by pointing
at it, his finger horned and bent.
High reverence in his gesture
suggests calamities yet to come
and death postponed, dreamt,
hungered for three-quarters of a century.

Mornings on the outskirts of Berlin
the days sidled over the edge of the world
nonchalant unto careless. He remembers
wondering why God did not care enough
to hurry, then fear of retribution
for his blasphemous thoughts.

The soldiers came in predawn dark
to carry away all he loved. The door
kicked in like a mouth. The apartment
ransacked. The sound of his father's head
on each wooden step as the soldiers descended.
His mother praying. Sister nightmare silent.

He points to the newborn sun as if they
have an inside joke about guilt, the kind
that fills a man when he can't sleep and so rises
to wait for the light—tardy just like in Berlin
when he was a boy—to finally touch his face.

The Prosecutor

A child's face and an old man's spotted hands,
he refuses to name the demon he serves
as he gesticulates his lies on the air. But Justice
he calls his bitch. He kicks her until she whimpers.
Shakespeare's offenseless dog abused to frighten
the imperious lion of Truth.

The prosecutor beats Justice unconscious. But she dreams
the lush plains of humanity as level as God's palm, a devouring
wind tight as God's fist in the tall grass. A wind with teeth.
This man's fear-mongering herd stampeding over the edge
of earth in the twilight. *Falling, falling, fallen.*

Justice's breathing, labored for the blood in her lungs,
on the prosecutor's brindled hand, is the tattered
music that makes this man smile. His voiced name
seven coughing ravens on the sky, bile on the tongue,
call note of unreason to silence songbirds.

His unspoken name a clicking lock, ringing chains,
the scraping of his black magician's unclean fingers
                                            at all our throats.

Money Song: The Totalized Capitalism Rag

There is money
on the sole of your shoe,
under your nails, caught
in your throat, staining
your kerchief if you sneeze.
You shit it, sing it, spread
it on bread for lunch.
Dream only of money
and swear oaths to it, by God.

Money, your life breath.
Money, your disease
and perfect coffin. Money
to get your book on a shelf, song
played, drug declared safe
no matter the side effects, bomb
dropped on hovels, shell
casings spilled over the ground
like holy water. Money
for your senator, your confessor,
so your ex will leave you alone.

Money at your head like a gun,
stuffed in your pants, up your ass,
so the border guards won't find it,
or under your mattress for a rainy day.
And hell, it won't quit raining. Money
dripping from your stiff upper lip, spilling
from your brown eyes, blue eyes,
eyes green like money. Money
to weigh you down, short-circuit
your synapses, drain your blood.

Money whose absence is the apocalypse,
its spectral-touch titillation and rebuke,
a badge to mark your insignificance, sign
of your unworthiness. Missing-money
nightmares every time you close your eyes,

dreams you dare not share for fear of banishment.

Money, money, money turns
the big prayer wheel, and so all good
children forget how to pray. Only
the losers remember, and they pray
for death to escape the icy touch,
the ghost-touch, of money.

The Naming

Poetry can repair no loss, but it defies the space that separates...
John Berger

You do not recognize the voice
as cinderblock echoes meet precisely
where you sit. Blindfolded. Piss-drenched.

The current flows better now
and you have almost grown accustomed
to the reek of boiled urine, singed
pubic hair, hot flesh...

Maybe it is not a voice at all, but rabbits
being slaughtered or hundreds of children
weeping or a nail driven through glass.

Strange to be embarrassed your tormenter
knows you so intimately, sees you this way,
smells you. Then shame gives way to emptiness
big as God: the rise and fall of the voice matches
the waves of pain inevitable as incoming tide.

And you open outward like a hothouse flower,
names rising like pollen on the scorched air:
your priest the vagabond urchins on your street
the man you met on the bus yesterday a librarian
you have only admired from afar the checker at the
market a neighbor's prepubescent child your dentist...

All innocent as far as you know, but you
can hate yourself tomorrow. The rest
of your life you can dream them screaming
in the same strained register as the cinderblock echoes.

Your tormentor removes the blindfold.
You blink to reveal a pair of bloodstained
panties, and the God-sized emptiness
fills with impossibly white sheet lightning.

80

You beg to die, but the tormentor asks patience,
cooperation. Just one more name so he can stop
hurting you, all this wailing and the mess
and the terrifying dreams he will have too. One
more name, so your daughter wife
sister can go free.

Tales of Persia

...we are the colonists of Death
Louis Simpson

The actual desert is as fiercely gorgeous
as Death, a goddess in sunlit copper
and sequins. But a cliché has entered
the collective soul of Westerners, a bad
American movie in black and white—all dust
and fear and a thirst that can't be slaked
even by blood—warping our dreams
with drab hues that must be answered.

Thus the hole, as long as half a football field,
is bathed in corpse-light, cinematically
pale, but the party guests are clothed
in deep earth tones for contrast. Much red,
much darkening purple leaking into the sand.

A minimalist dance center scene: a twitch
here, a look of profound surprise over there
as the D-9 made-in-America—a man
at the controls in fatigues and Stetson, keffiyeh,
yarmulke to honor his God, ball cap emblazoned
with Nike swoosh, Yankees, Patriots, Man United—
pushes backfill, spouts black smoke against a virgin sky.

The watcher knows the party will continue
in the dark, the mute revelers playing games:
who can turn to bone quickest, remember
their name longest, dream the worse revenge
and get a message through to their kin
still above ground using the bleak telepathy
the massacred learn down here, in a trench
in the actual desert, in the utter night turned colder
than any gone before.

But we are not shown, and fail to imagine,
the mourners stage right, children putting on the robes
of orphanhood, the staggering for want of limbs.

The hole in the fabric of the world left by every corpse:
a thousand songs missing, a hundred paintings,
a good poem or two. Maybe an algorithm for finding
anything lost. Maybe a ceremony to set it all right.

About the Author

MICHAEL MCIRVIN was born in the Nebraska Panhandle in 1956. He taught writing and literature for many years at various institutions, including Colorado State University and the University of Wyoming, and for the past several years he has been a freelance editor and writing mentor. His poems, stories, essays, and book reviews have appeared in hundreds of periodicals, and he is the author of nine books: poetry collections, novels, and an essay collection. He lives on the High Plains of Wyoming with his wife Sharon and is currently writing another novel.